Dancing with Dali

ᏀᏀᏀ

MAUREEN SHERBONDY

FUTURECYCLE PRESS
www.futurecycle.org

Cover artwork, "Field with Poppies" by Vincent Van Gogh; author photo by Zachary Sherbondy; cover and interior book design by Diane Kistner; Gentium Basic text and Kefa titling

Library of Congress Control Number: 2019949978

Published by FutureCycle Press
Athens, Georgia, USA

ISBN 978-1-942371-81-6

For Barry

Contents

DANCING WITH DALI

Summer Wasteland

A clear demarcation exists
between blue uncertainty
and sandy beach.
Here, sky is ocean
and ocean, clouds.

This is not the pearl
sanctuary of summer
but a graveyard
without burial. No coffin
exists for the headless woman.

Do not ask where are
her feet, her hands.
Do not ask why
the dog died.

Some cruel architect
of the sand carved
out a reverse castle—
indentation of square
and chimney, natural
container to capture
red-orange blood.

Her giant head floats
between two places
facing its body
with closed eyes.
We turn away
from our own end.

The only living creatures
that remain are seven
blood-red fish swimming
on the blue side, oblivious
to death waiting on land.

Dancing with Dali

His hands grow too large
and swallow my palms
as we attempt to waltz
across the desert.

Odd items fly overhead—
a melting clock, elephants
and swans, a seated Madonna.

"It is all about desire," he sings
in my ears (now turning into bees).

Behind a skeleton tree, Magritte
hides in the drawers
of an armoire, his face covered
by an apple. A brush
in his hand paints our dance.

I imagine the image of us
will be forever blocked by a hat.

My attention now turns to Dali,
who is swirling away,
dancing instead with Marilyn's
lip-couch, waltzing through the desert
until the dwindling speck of cadmium vanishes.

Beach Scene of Obsolescence

A rotary phone receiver, once cradled
between the warm shoulder
and ear of a chatty teen,
now waits like a jilted lover
for soft lips to release words
and reach a person on the other side
of a line sliced away
from all communication.

In the desert landscape of obsolescence,
beside this phone
the dot-matrix printer
sees dots day and night
but has no paper to imprint
with words. Floppy disks
lie on the sand like dead fish
brought in with the old tide,
tossed aside for fresher catch.

8-track tape players
sing their slow, deep dirges
into the dunes. Songs cry out
into the nightmares of the tap-
tap-tapping typewriters. Old keys
touch the worn-out, inkless
ribbons. Carbon paper copies
SOS on rocks and sand, waiting
for 727 jets to land and rescue them.

Frozen Clock

It is so hot in the South
that time melts away;
the clock folds into itself.

As a child it seemed
I could freeze the hours.
My mother would remain forty,
moving as fast as a NASCAR race car
and healthy for eternity.

My father would continue mowing
the lawn through summer's wilting grass,
his shirt drenched in Saturday sweat,

while ants crawled at a snail's pace
up and down their slow-built mound.
The yard is now a concrete lawn.

My mother's heart races, her fastest
movement these days. The anthills
have long since flattened out.

My own hair grows quickly gray
and the only thing frozen in time—
my father's heart and body stopped
and still beneath this heated ground.

Needle and Thread

Nothing is whole in this place
of heat and desolation.
She wants to mend scattered
parts together, to thread the stars
into a necklace of luminosity.

In the desert now, she removes
the giant needle from her bag,
then finds a spool of silver thread.
The woman sews the head back on the torso.

At night the seamed face bends
toward her. Muttering mouth noises
guide her to the hollow man's land.
Road signs read *Dali lives here.*

Fried Eggs

Two eggs fried on a plate;
one's fate is dangling by a thread.

My own eggs age and leave
this body bed.

Once three eggs formed into three sons;
now the highway of my female anatomy

has turned away from me, inflamed
with grapefruits on every underpass.

One day it will be sluiced away—
the end of female days. And the eggs

will be an echo of baby
cries in an ancient cave.

After Soft Watches

The Camembert is melting;
the Gouda runs away;
chocolate turns into
a muddled puddle of sweetness.

Smear the cheese on your tongue,
chocolate on your hand like paint.
It is all about the melting in this heat.
Memory drifts, returning
in a different form anyway.

Winter will come again to freeze
these bones, these foods, to solidify
your new perception of this heated fodder.

Six Apparitions of Lenin

Have a cherry, Mr. Lenin.
Oh, I know it's you—
six glowing faces rising
in sunny halos from piano keys.

A door is open. It's not too late
for leaving or revolution.

Hold on to the chair for
your dear life, then watch notes
and ants dance
on music and history books.

Self-Portrait with Necklace of Thorns

The monkey sits on her shoulder
tying vines in the shape of a necklace.
A black cat on the other shoulder
waits to pounce on a black bird
that dangles from the necklace twig.

And Frida stares out to the distance,
still and silent, as if there is not
a single thing she can do. One slight
movement and a thorny branch blade
might slit her throat. Once hurt, she now
expects the universe to deliver only pain.

The Artist

I wanted to paint like my older brother.
I created sienna swollen-thick lines
on canvas. Thin attempts
at cadmium yellow fruit in failed
crimson half-circular bowls, then
on to cartoonish suns and moons.

All symbols for what I desired
to know and show to others. I cried
when turpentine fumes sent me
into a spell of dizzy confusion
away from the brush and oil paints.

Now, through words instead, I am
still trying to invoke the sun
and moon as I lie down, stare at glowing
unattainable figures. All metaphors at best.
While my brother conjured his forests so real,
he has wandered off the canvas edge
and become lost inside the painted woods.

Painting at the North Carolina Museum of Art

There is something wrong
with the painting.
Even before I read the side caption,
I see it. The wife, too stiff, out of place,
is the hole in the painting, the missing
piece shoved in to make it
complete, only it is not.

She is staring beyond the artist, caught
in a limbo place we cannot see
or imagine between death and dying
while the husband stands, happy at the thought
of family complete—the cherubs,
pink-cheeked lively children in fancy dress,
stuck in a permanent state of bliss
as if they do not know
the mother is not really there.

I imagine him coming home
hapless-faced, realizing
she is not there anymore,
her side of the bed left
flat, unwrinkled.

I see him looking up at the
painting, believing if he stares
at her brush-stroked face
long enough, she will appear
in flesh in front of him.

Pear

Well, why not? So much depended
on a single lush plum. Take a pear
this time, paint it larger. In a child's
mind, hunger for the fruit makes
it essential. In the girl's world, proportion
shifts off-kilter. A colossal pear reaches
the sky and clouds. Throw in
some fish removed from the bowl;
let them float by like fireflies.
That dwarf elephant holds
out a trunk like a hand. The girl
reaches for it. She will create and grab
every single vision she desires.

Hands

Hands grow so large, they weigh
her body down. Walking becomes
arms dragging behind, hands pulling
piles of dirt and stones like a rake.

Heavy burden that defies proportion
and logic. She befriends the dog
with the giant ears and the boy
with that too-large pointed nose.

When people make fun
of her, she threatens to slap them
silly with those fists. They flee.

She dreams of the Giant
and the Beanstalk, but all
she desires in the morning
is proportion or waking
up in a cockroach's thorax.

Journey

The old house hovers over
the ocean; fish drift across
clouds. Do not ask how
they swim through air.
Movement isn't always logical.
Sometimes a man runs
when no one is chasing him.

You might ask how do residents
from the water house go
to and fro? Sea to land
and land to sea. Maybe no humans
live inside, and it's all part
of house as greenery. Living
quarters just for birds and squirrels.

Swim through the waves, then hold
your breath and dive inside watery
imagination. Nothing is as it should be.
Why shouldn't fish fly, and why
shouldn't an old house appear in an ocean tree?

Tilled Field

Here in the Catalonian field
between vertical swivels
and horizontal lines, mine
for animals: a forward-facing
dog, a tail-swooshing horse,
a rooster, more dogs, and a snail.

An ear leaning on a tree listens
to voices from the one house.
Perhaps occupants fear wandering
across the animal-filled tilled field.

Danger waits everywhere—sharp
blades slice the yellow sky,
and an all-knowing eye
watches from that single tree.

Dorothy in Paris

At the Musée d'Orsay
Dorothy clicks her red heels
together three times.
In front of Monet's *Regattas at Argenteuil*
she expects to float
into pastoral waters, to sail into the wall of
oil on canvas, tranquil pastels.

The docent yells in French
not to lean so close,
but the language barrier
precludes action. When three guards
usher her out to the street
she gets the point.
You're not in Kansas, Aunt Em's voice
whispers in her ears. *Not even in the USA.*

She taps her heels together again,
wanting to fly home but feeling
scattered, ends up at a patisserie
devouring croissants, pastries,
and sorrow beneath cigarette
smoke and foreign chatter.

Museum of Lost Wishes

Enter the museum of wishes; clutch
a star and let it burn your hand. Release
it; watch it swish and twirl across
the air, then travel room to room.

At night the janitor hums and runs his broom
along the floor, then gathers crumbs
of disappointment, dots of accumulated yearning.
He spills burnt ash remnants in the trash.

What will you learn here? Release
all that you once desired; spit honey
from your tongue. Your lovers
left you years before. All turns bitter,

then wooden-framed. Your heart no longer pumps
with blood or want. God-painted cells harden.
In the end there is just a metal plaque
nailed on the museum wall marking

your single masterpiece now on display.
Colored places and faces you never found.
That janitor will return to sweep away
any clues or crumbs you left behind.

Hiding in Plain Sight

"A Rodin Hiding in Plain Sight in a New Jersey Suburb"
Newspaper headline, October 2017

The Rodin sculpture collects
nothing but dust, no appreciative stares.
A white marble Napoleon bust sits
in a corner of a room on the second floor
of the Madison Borough Council
hall. On black and white floors, the bust rests
on a pedestal that's used as a leaning post between
meetings where council members
debate and discuss taxes, zoning,
and budgets. The white walls stare
artless and dull at the white bust.
It's as if a stunning teenager
behind the grocery register waits
unnoticed by hordes of shoppers,
until one day a casting agent arrives
and recognizes her unique beauty.

The Broken Column

This body is now more machine
than human circuitry. While metal
reconstructs my spine, how can I
bend as I once did? Take your nail,
carpenter, machinist, O great builder,
doctor man. Make me new again,
upright and functioning. Why
can't you stop the transmittal
of pain from registering in my
human and vulnerable brain?

If Picasso Worked in the Mall Food Court

Of course he flirts with all the women—
young mothers pushing strollers,
twenty-year-old blonde Neiman Marcus sales clerks
dressed in Donna Karan or Valentino.
He draws them naked in his mind,

whistles while he sweeps up pizza
crust, French fries, chicken nuggets.
The spills of milkshakes and cola
he eagerly anticipates so he can swipe
the mop strands through, brush-like,

creating art of pink, white, and brown
liquid collages on linoleum canvas
with no sense of permanence—a slipping hazard
for passersby who might not make aesthetic sense
of the swirls and swivels. Danger he knows,
so he sets down the orange cones.

He hopes one day to be recognized
for creating rather than erasing amidst the daily throwing
out and cleaning up of waste that from
the right perspective might become a work of art.
He dreams these same mall patrons will place his future
paintings in their cart instead of shoes and scarves.

Without the Accident

And what if the accident
never occurred? Frida
might have painted dull
landscapes or dog portraits.
Without pain and convalescence,
she'd have been just another
unnoticed artist, her canvases sold
at garage sales or abandoned
in attics far from any pain or fame.

Vincent Van Gogh's Ear

What became of that ear once sliced away,
the lopped-off lobe, the folds of skin and cartilage?
Did he grind it into paint to create
an eerie-eary canvas? Or perhaps he set it free—
after handing it to Rachel at the brothel,
did she, in turn, toss the ear out to sea? Floating bulbously
on some untamed body of water—across the River Thames,
no-name sailboat without a sail, fleshy canoe
without oars, unveiled for all the fish and passersby to see.

What did it hear when pressed against the water's
surface? Sound of life and death beneath. Rush
of depth and breath, the swishing and sloshing of plants and fish.
Did the ear hear land while on water, the sound of its master
painting as it sailed across the amputated hours?

Or was it really lost in a sword fight with Gauguin?
Van Gogh hushing up the truth out of loyalty to his friend,
defending him by letting the world believe
for over a century in Van Gogh's insanity to save
the other artist's reputation and paint an everlasting
world vision. Mouth to ear and mouth to ear, we hear
his creative temperament turned permanent—crazy artiste.

Dali TV

In the television universe
of the Dali satellite service
I view abstract palettes
shifting across the screen
in hues of blues, greens,
and colors in-between.

CNN anchors have two misshapen
heads; they sit at broken-legged
desks plopped down in the desert.
Beside them is a melting clock
spewing stock ticker-tape
coated in ant parades.

The Marilyn Monroe lips sofa
rests in a corner, waiting
for political guests—
skulls of men and women
who will comment on giant heads
that have overtaken Congress
while elephants march
across the golden screen, stomping
out noise from mouthy machines.

Red

So much red.
Not Vincent Van Gogh's poppies
this time: rows
of cheerful red flowers looking up
to the spired tree-filled sky.
No, not red poppies in a field
but red faces against church pews,
prayers startled on lips, bodies
slumped over.
Texas parishioners walk into a church
but never get to leave.
What good is that row of flowers
that no one gets to see?

THE ART OF DISTRACTION

The Art of Distraction

Tap-dance on a table; sing
an off-key rendition of *The Star-Spangled Banner*;
point to the fat man in another country
or a donkey tripping in the woods.

Build a circus tent near a white house;
fill it with clever rhetoric from
shameful clowns who hide behind masks
of meteoric blame, painted-on smiles,
shifty eyes. Here, trapeze artists throw

bodies and excuses across hot air.
Distract the crowd often, as our parents
once did when we were children.
Set an innocent ex-candidate on stage
and watch as elephants trample her.

Bust of a Woman

Pose with bread on your head
like a hat, a balancing act
of a man and a maid beside
the toilet and a bin for laundry
and a pen. Stare out beyond
the framed air while ants
race up your face, parade
near your ear and on the
rising road of your lip while
monkey-like men dance
on your collar necklace
and the harvest rests
on your neck in a scarf
of corn, husked and tied
from behind. No discourse
here but balance and oddity
merged on a bust waiting
to be noticed and understood.

The Lovers

O, lover, we can never
meld as we really desire—
to be you inside of me
and me inside of you
lastingly. If I could,
I would place you within
my veins to flow up
and down as the moon
waxes and wanes.

But no,
we are separate and covered
in fabric masks, hidden,
revealing only the voices
and actions we choose
to disclose.
Our glitches, our flaws
remain concealed in this
glossy outerwear of skin, cloth.

At the Dali Furniture Store

The customer wanders through
rows of armoires, dressers, and beds.
He stops before a statue of a woman
standing tall with two drawers, one
jutting out from her stomach, one
from her teak breasts. Metal nipples
as pulls. He takes her home,
thrilled to have both female companion
and a place to store his clothes.

Word Collage in the Museum

Set Scrabble tiles inside
the perimeter, along with the alphabet
letters from the top of Miss Johnson's
first-grade classroom. A to Z from you to me.
There for the taking. I will steal
them in coffee shops,
restaurants, and gas stations.
Rearrange them in a whim
of decision and indecision.
As soon as you release ramblings
into the free public space,
I will gather and set them
inside the wooden frame hanging
on the wall of the found-word museum.

My Wife, the Found Poet

2 a.m. The mess of it,
as if a stray panther
leaped through the window,
shred the books with
her claws. She looked
up at me, purring,
a ten-line found poem
set on the floor before her,
leftover words spilling
from the corners of her lips.

Beneath the Water

You see only the half of me
that you want to see.
Much goes on beneath water—
whiskered fish drift by;
rocks pave a path
for creatures to walk on.

And the chair I set my hand
upon, you can't see that either.
Strength waits below.
I have leaned on the invisible
my entire life. I wade
between two worlds—
the river and hard land.

The earliest memory
swims to me in dreams.
I recall the seams
of my mother's uterus;
here I swam without
breathing oxygen
from the blue-sky world.

I want to go back
to the sack of water,
but now these lungs
require air and land.
Look at me. You will never
see the struggles waiting beneath.

Lobster Telephone

She picks up the telephone
to hear the sea; you see
the call comes in by way
of lobster circuitry.

As in sea creature.
No one knows how dinner
landed on that receiver top.
When she picked it up
on the ring ring third
ring, her ear got pinched
by that elongated thing.

Pick up a shell to hear the sea;
the lobster entity only
elicits pain and memory.

Women Forming a Skull

We are capable of everything—
plowing a field, cooking cakes
and stews, brewing coffee, tea,
working inside offices in cities and towns,
creating life from inside out.

Here, too, we stand on each other's
shoulders, lifting our naked bodies,
our arms, bending and adapting;
we surround flesh to shape
our combined selves into a single skull,

hollowed selves both welcoming
and frightening visitors.

Golconda

Where is Mary Poppins and her famous umbrella?
Office-less men in suits fall from the sky, torpedo-like
and ready for war or taxes, black specks like flies.
Perfectly straight, rule followers, upright and ready
in their overcoat containers, robotic conformists without
    commander.

Dada

Yes, yes, go on
Mr. Hobby Horse:
color in outside the lines;
shock me into motion and stillness.

Draw outside the framed frame
the box, a box,
a rectangle, and a hook—
perhaps a button
to unbutton nothing and everything.

Place a hook inside it;
hold it up from the sky;
question everything
then nothing.

Life is not
no no.

Numbered Days

Your entire body is built by days—
day in and day out, day of disaster,
defeat or interludes in the dusty heat.
Hold up your arm to recall
the tenth of June when you pitched
a perfect game. A year later
the other hand caught flame
in the backyard barbecue. Then
your lame legs became weighed
down by the two-by-two cubicle
of work monotony—a nine-to-five
daily ritual of coming and going
by train. Thirty inane years of living
on weekends only. Soon all numbers
will blow away in the winter wind
and so, my dear friend, will you.

The Art of Distraction II

Distraction does not detract
in any way from day or night.
Mind grows wings, tunes out
teachers chattering, parents jabbering.

While children shout across the street, this one
girl sings. She rests atop a blanket of gray flowers
and yellow background; she hears the humming sound
of bees and the music playing inside her head.

There is a symphony within, an orchestra
replete with violin, harp, flute, and clarinet.
It suits her well, this mini-world
she travels to whenever the wicked exterior
becomes too much for her to endure.

Radium Girl

Novelty, it was, so I painted my nails
and giggled as radiance lit up the room.
I passed chirpy gossip of boyfriends
to my factory friends while brushing on
numbered clock faces so time would be visible
in the darkest places for customers.

Liquid radium. I didn't know it was poison
soaking through my skin and bones.
Years later, what once blazed gold
spilled inside my blood, became sickness.

Who will pay for such novelty, malady,
this breaking of bones, disintegration
of body, of time? How can it be
that what once glowed brightly
has turned so dark, so final?

I Do Not Live There

I do not live in your world
of neat, lined highways
and green fields.

Two exits down
from expectation
you will find me

quiescent beneath the giant
pear. Here where
rain is blood
and blood is gin.

I swim laps in a river
of daisies and roses;
thorns sluice skin.

My mouth soothes
every cut, and now
liquor leaks from pores
and ragged ruts.

Do not talk in melodic niceties;
giant ears from the elephant
have no patience for
level banter. Fight and yell instead,

or sew shut those cherry lips.
Rest beneath the pear.
When hunger rises,
tear open thread and bite.

La Grande Guerre

Cover my features with purple
flowers surrounded by green leaves.
Dress me in white so I become
merely mannequin, bride
with no groom, painted woman
with no soul. The allies of sea
and sky—my eternal backdrop.

Like a tan brick wall, I stand
as posed object, tall as clouds,
statue before water and watcher;
my arm becomes only a hook
for that single prop—a gray purse.

The Patio Creation

The making of the patio is progressing
rather slowly. Workers set a frame too small
and low to satisfy the size requirements
clearly stated in the builder's contract.

I watch the new-poured rectangle with growing
animosity, sludge flowing forth like batter.
Observing as it dries, solidifies,
I notify the man in charge of men,
wondering if maybe the workmen
interpreted 12 as 2 instead. They ought
to learn to measure properly.

Three times now they've ripped up
the shape, dragged away the corpse
of shame, error of cracked cake,
then left behind a muddy mess
for the neighborhood to witness
this construction digression.

Torn grass and so much ragged earth
exists in this war zone of incompetence.
The making of the patio is turning
into quite a show while profit
for the man deteriorates with every new mistake.
The next time they attempt another crass
rebuild, I'll leave keepsakes in the yard
so in the end it turns out right
with my gift of measuring tape and glasses.

A Plot

It was about
a man and a woman
falling in love.
No, it was about
a man and a woman divorcing
and a son who ran from home
to join the circus or the army
or the sales force at Cisco.
There was a death, a funeral,
a wedding. Things happened.
People settled on a plot
of land. Holes were dug;
someone fell in. An artist appeared
and painted it all away.

Elephant Celebes

Over here, Mr. Elephant.
Yes, I am faceless, but still a voice
stirs and finds your sharp bull horns.

Fish fly as birds once did
and voice is given to the dead,
though they too lack lips.

I have no head, no mouth,
but these metal arms
manage to guide you here.

Terrible Dictators

Sometimes a giant rooster
takes over the mountain.

Call him animal, call him
dictator; both labels fit.

The squawking is the same;
it leads to a common endgame.

Years later, when guns are locked
away, nameless corpses rise.

A rooster hides behind every hill;
weak ears wander, then follow him.

Ubu Imperator

Upside-down birdhouse
walking on a needle
to make a point in dirt—
stagnation. Blow at the clouds
and stand posing.

The cloud has fallen into
a swirled scarf that rests
wrapped around your torso.

No birds will enter your hollow
eye while those pasty white hands
wait to grab their feathered wings.

Death and the Miser

And where did greed ever lead
the merchant anyway? Years
he spent accumulating gold coins
in a sack, then hiding them inside
the locked chest, never giving
back with love or charity.
Does special treatment arrive in the end
for men with an abundance of wealth?

He reclines skeleton-like
in his penultimate role as patient,
thin and pale, infirm, waiting in the
hospice suite. His former vibrant self
stands opposite, taunting, demons
surrounding the bed and lustful
death creaking open the door.

Even now, when a shady creature
offers that bag replete with riches,
the dying man reaches shamelessly
instead of noticing the window-square
section of Christ, streaming light
pouring embers of redemption
in his direction. Why must he once again
ignore the angel's gentle suggestion?

And why does he in these final seconds
draw his hand instead
toward avarice when no velvet
robes or ruby-encrusted
gold crowns will accompany
any man to that eternal nether land?

The Tactile Memory of Clay

As a child I dug clay
from a stream with my bare
hands, then shaped the lump
into figures—
a cat, a child, a bird.

Now daily on the broken-lined
highway to work I ask, *What do I build?*
In my office I fill paper
blanks with ink, type letters
into forms on screens.
In rooms I release gestures,
words, then my hands dangle empty.

Most days, lessons vanish, fly
out open windows, away
from twenty pairs of ears,
little sediment settling
at the base of those live streams.

But then today one student announces,
*My friend said you helped him become
a better writer.* My palms
begin to itch, open up like flowers,
as if his words dug up that old found
clay, set the familiar shape inside
my patient, waiting hands.

Notes

Certain poems were based on specific images from various artists, including:

"Frozen Clock": Salvador Dali's "The Persistence of Memory"

"Six Apparitions of Lenin": Salvador Dali's "Six Apparitions of Lenin on a Grand Piano"

"Self-Portrait with Necklace of Thorns": Frida Kahlo's "Self-Portrait with Thorn Necklace and Hummingbird"

"Pear": Nikolina Petolas's "Passing Strangers"

"Journey": Nikolina Petolas's "Journey"

"The Broken Column": Frida Kahlo's "The Broken Column"

"Bust of a Woman": Salvador Dali's "Retrospective Bust of a Woman"

"The Lovers": René Magritte's "The Lovers"

"Beneath the Water": Laura Christensen's "Muse"

"Lobster Telephone": Salvador Dali's "Lobster Telephone"

"Women Forming a Skull": Salvador Dali's "Women Forming a Skull"

"Golconda": René Magritte's "Golconda"

"Numbered Days": Harry Wilson's "Days in San Francisco #1, 1984"

"La Grande Guerre": René Magritte's "La Grande Guerre"

"Elephant Celebes": Max Ernst's "The Elephant Celebes"

"Ubu Imperator": Max Ernst's "Ubu Imperator"

"Death and the Miser": Hieronymus Bosch's "Death and the Miser"

"Painting at the North Carolina Museum of Art": John Singleton Copley's "Sir William Pepperell and His Family"

Acknowledgments

100 Word Story: "Radium Girl"
Broad River Review: "If Picasso Worked at the Mall Food Court"
Crucible: "Painting at the North Carolina Museum of Art"
Ekphrastic Review: "Bust of a Woman"
Indianapolis Review: "Frozen Clock"
Jet Fuel Review: "The Artist"

"Dorothy in Paris" appeared in the chapbook *After the Fairy Tale* (Main Street Rag, 2007).

About FutureCycle Press

FutureCycle Press is dedicated to publishing lasting English-language poetry books, chapbooks, and anthologies in both print-on-demand and Kindle ebook formats. Founded in 2007 by long-time independent editor/publishers and partners Diane Kistner and Robert S. King, the press incorporated as a nonprofit in 2012. A number of our editors are distinguished poets and writers in their own right, and we have been actively involved in the small press movement going back to the early seventies.

The FutureCycle Poetry Book Prize and honorarium is awarded annually for the best full-length volume of poetry we publish in a calendar year. Introduced in 2013, our Good Works projects are anthologies devoted to issues of universal significance, with all proceeds donated to a related worthy cause. Our Selected Poems series highlights contemporary poets with a substantial body of work to their credit; with this series we strive to resurrect work that has had limited distribution and is now out of print.

We are dedicated to giving all of the authors we publish the care their work deserves, making our catalog of titles the most diverse and distinguished it can be, and paying forward any earnings to fund more great books.

We've learned a few things about independent publishing over the years. We've also evolved a unique, resilient publishing model that allows us to focus mainly on vetting and preserving for posterity poetry collections of exceptional quality without becoming overwhelmed with bookkeeping and mailing, fundraising activities, or taxing editorial and production "bubbles." To find out more about what we are doing, come see us at www.futurecycle.org.

The FutureCycle Poetry Book Prize

All full-length volumes of poetry published by FutureCycle Press in a given calendar year are considered for the annual FutureCycle Poetry Book Prize. This allows us to consider each submission on its own merits, outside of the context of a contest. Too, the judges see the finished book, which will have benefitted from the beautiful book design and strong editorial gloss we are famous for.

The book ranked the best in judging is announced as the prize-winner in the subsequent year. There is no fixed monetary award; instead, the winning poet receives an honorarium of 20% of the total net royalties from all poetry books and chapbooks the press sold online in the year the winning book was published. The winner is also accorded the honor of being on the panel of judges for the next year's competition; all judges receive copies of all contending books to keep for their personal library.

Made in the USA
Columbia, SC
07 February 2020